Helen canham

Helen canham

THREE GOLDEN RAINBOWS

The people of Tibet dearly love and respect their leader, the Dalai Lama. When each Dalai Lama dies, his love for his people lives on and returns to earth in the form of the child who is the next Dalai Lama.

When the thirteenth Dalai Lama died, the people of Tibet were sad, for he had been a very wise ruler. But they knew that somewhere in their country they would find the special child who would be the fourteenth Dalai Lama.

No one knew who this child was or where he would be found — but they did know that a trail of magic signs would lead the searchers to him.

This is the story of that search . . .

I thank Wendy Paton of the Australian-Tibetan Society and Lama Tubten Choedak for their assistance and encouragement during the preparation of this book.

First published in 1989 by
Hodder & Stoughton (Australia) Pty Ltd
10-16 South Street, Rydalmere, NSW, 2116

National Library of Australia Cataloguing-in-Publication entry
Claire, Stephanie.
    Three golden rainbows
    ISBN 0 340 41933 4.
    I. Zofrea, Salvatore, 1946-   . II. Title.
A823'.3

Typeset in 15/18 Clearface by Love Computer Typesetting Pty Ltd, Sydney, Australia.
Printed in Hong Kong

THREE GOLDEN RAINBOWS

Stephanie Claire

Salvatore Zofrea

HODDER AND STOUGHTON
SYDNEY AUCKLAND LONDON TORONTO

In the monastery courtyard six boys, their heads bent in prayer, were waiting for their teacher. Outside, even the market place was still as the people of Lhasa honoured the death of their thirteenth Dalai Lama.

"Where is Gen-la?" Tashi whispered to his friend Gyalpo, then quickly went on praying as he heard the sound of footsteps.

A moment later the courtyard gate clicked open and their teacher Gen-la hurried in, clutching his orange robes round him for warmth.

The boys stopped praying and looked up.

"May you soon be enlightened," Gen-la greeted them, as he always did at the start of the day. Then he began the lesson.

"You all know that ever since our Dalai Lama died, we have offered prayers for him and guarded his body at the Summer Palace. But we must do something more . . ." He looked round the class.

Gyalpo put up his hand and bowed to his teacher. "We must pray for the special child who is our next Dalai Lama," he said.

"Yes, Gyalpo, — you are right," Gen-la replied. "With the death of our Dalai Lama, Tibet has entered unusual times and until we find this child we will see and hear many strange things."

Just as he finished speaking there came a loud banging on the gate and three excited lamas burst into the courtyard.

"Gen-la," their leader said, bowing. "Forgive us for interrupting your class, but we have some strange and wonderful news — may we tell you?"

"Yes of course," Gen-la answered.

"As you know," the lama began, "every night the Dalai Lama's body at the Summer Palace is guarded very carefully. This morning at dawn, one of the guards entered the room where his body was and another went out to check the palace grounds. Very soon, they both came running back . . ."

"Why? What had happened?" Gen-la asked, leaning forward intently.

"I will tell you," said the lama slowly, looking round the courtyard at his audience. "Late last night when the guard made his check, the Dalai Lama's head was facing the south. But when that guard entered the room early this morning, he saw that his head no longer faced the south — now, it was facing the north-east!" He paused to enjoy the effect of his words.

The six boys stared at each other in amazement, then turned and looked at Gen-la.

"Continue," Gen-la said impatiently. "What about the other guard — why did *he* come running back?"

"Ah, yes . . . the other guard," said the lama, stringing out his story as long as he could. "First, he checked the west side of the palace — all quiet; then he walked along the north side — all quiet there too . . . but as he rounded

the next corner, a bird came swooping down out of the sky and almost landed on his head. Of course, he looked up — and then he saw that overnight, on the corner of the palace roof . . . a huge star-shaped mushroom had grown."

The boys' eyes widened with excitement. No one spoke.

Gen-la thought for a moment then he said, "If the guard walked along the west side of the Palace and then along the north side, the next corner he came to would face the . . .?"

"East!" the boys cried together.

Gen-la shook his head. "Nearly right, but not quite," he said. "Think again".

Tashi put up his hand. He stood up and bowed to his teacher. "Gen-la, I think the next corner would face the north-east."

"Correct," Gen-la nodded. "And now, Tashi, can you tell us what these strange events might mean?"

Tashi thought for a moment, then gave his answer. "During the night the Dalai Lama's head turned to face the north-east, and the star-shaped mushroom grew on the north-east corner of the Summer Palace. Maybe these are signs that the boy who is our next Dalai Lama will be found in the north-east part of Tibet." He bowed again and sat down.

The three lamas nodded solemnly.

"Yes, Tashi," Gen-la replied, "you may well be right".

He glanced up at the bright morning sun which now warmed the courtyard. "I will let you all have a holiday today. Why don't you go to the Summer Palace and see for yourselves this giant mushroom?"

At this, the boys leapt to their feet, bowed and rushed out the courtyard gate. With a thoughtful look on his face, Gen-la crossed over to the gate and closed it behind them.

8

As they hurried along the path that led to the Summer Palace, the boys talked about the star-shaped mushroom.

"I wonder how big it is," said Gyalpo.

"Pretty large, I should think," Tashi replied. "After all, a sign must be big enough for the people to see."

When they reached the main gates of the Summer Palace they could see that news of the strange mushroom had spread. It seemed that everyone in the city of Lhasa had stopped work to go and see it.

A huge crowd blocked their way.

"This is hopeless," said Gyalpo in dismay. "We'll never get close enough to see it properly . . . Let's try another entrance."

Just as Tashi turned to answer him, his eye was caught by something in the sky. He looked again and there, arching high above the city, were *three golden rainbows*.

He stood still, gazing up at them. Never in his life had he seen anything so strange and beautiful. Then he felt Gyalpo tug at his sleeve.

"Hey, Tashi!" he was saying. "Hurry up, the others are waiting for us."

As if in a dream, Tashi pointed upwards. "Look, Gyalpo," he said wonderingly, "look at those rainbows — aren't they strange . . . ?"

Gyalpo looked up at the sky, then at Tashi. "What are you talking about?" he said, puzzled. "I can't see anything."

The three golden rainbows had disappeared.

Tashi closed his eyes, trying to hold on to their image.

Now Gyalpo was getting impatient. "Come on, Tashi," he was saying, "if we don't look out, we'll lose the others in the crowd".

Suddenly Tashi knew what he must do. "You go with the others," he said. "I must go back to Gen-la and tell him what I've seen."

He weaved his way through the crowd and ran back along the path. By the time he reached the monastery, he was quite tired out. With his last breath, he ran across the courtyard and knocked at the big wooden door.

After a moment, the door was opened by Gen-la. "What are you doing back here, Tashi?" he asked. "I thought you boys had all gone to the Summer Palace."

Tashi took a deep breath. "We did go there, Gen-la," he said, "and the others are still there. But I had to come back".

"Why?" Gen-la asked, looking at him closely. "What made you come back?"

"I think I may have seen a sign," Tashi replied. "Something made me look up, and I saw three beautiful golden rainbows in the sky. They hung there for just a moment, then faded away. Gyalpo was with me — but he didn't see them at all."

"Where in the sky did you see these rainbows?" Gen-la asked quietly.

Tashi pointed.

"Ah . . . as I thought," Gen-la murmured looking at Tashi thoughtfully. "In the north-east. Wait here — I'll be back very soon," and he disappeared into the monastery.

A few minutes later the big wooden door opened again and Gen-la emerged followed by two other lamas. Tashi was asked to tell his story again and when he'd finished the two other lamas spoke briefly with Gen-la.

They went back inside and Gen-la sat down in the courtyard with Tashi. "Those two lamas agree that what you have seen is another sign — and they have gone to inform the Regent of it."

"The Regent!" Tashi exclaimed. The Regent was very important. Until the next Dalai Lama was found and grew up, it was the Regent who would rule the country.

"Yes," Gen-la replied. "We must tell the Regent, for he will know when the time is right to begin the search for this special child. And now," he added, "you must go and find your friends and enjoy the rest of the day."

Two whole years went by. Each day, Tashi and the other boys attended their school in the monastery courtyard. They studied hard, for later on they would be lamas too.

Sometimes Tashi thought about the star-shaped mushroom and the three golden rainbows and the special child living somewhere in Tibet.

One afternoon towards the end of winter, Gen-la asked him to stay behind when class had finished.

"Tashi," he said. "The time has now come to begin the search for the child who is our new Dalai Lama. The government has ordered that search-parties be sent out all over Tibet."

"Are you going to join in the search, Gen-la?"

"Yes," Gen-la replied. "Our monastery is sending a search-party and we will leave tomorrow morning at dawn."

"Who will be in the search-party?" Tashi asked.

"Just four of us — Lama Kewtsang Rinpoché, his assistant, myself and . . ."

"And who?"

"You, Tashi," Gen-la replied. "Because you saw the sign of the three golden rainbows in the north-east sky, you are to join us on our search."

Tashi just sat there. He could not believe his good fortune.

Then Gen-la said, "Go and find your friends and tell them your news. Enjoy the rest of the day with them, for it will be a long time before you see them again."

The next morning, Tashi was up before sunrise. He put on the thick, warm clothes he'd been given for the journey and went outside to look for Gen-la.

There, a strange sight met his eyes. Crowded into the shadowy courtyard were three fierce-looking men on horseback, all wearing big fur hats. In the corner, a black

yak piled high with stores and baggage waited patiently,
and by his side stood a sturdy brown pony.

When the merchants saw Tashi standing there, one of

them came over to him and took off his furry hat.

"Gen-la!" Tashi exclaimed. "Why are you dressed up like this? I didn't know you!"

Gen-la laughed. "It is better for us to travel dressed as merchants — this way, we won't attract attention."

Tashi looked carefully at the other two merchants, then asked in a low voice, "And are those other men . . . ?"

"Yes," answered Gen-la, "Lama Kewtsang and his assistant. When they take off their hats, you will see that they, too, have shaven heads. Now I will take you to meet them."

After introducing Tashi, Gen-la tied his bag with all the other baggage on to the back of the big black yak whose name was Norbu.

By this time, all the other lamas in the monastery had gathered in the courtyard to wave goodbye to the search-party.

Tashi climbed up on to the brown pony.

"Good luck, Tashi!" his friends called. "We will be thinking of you . . . we wish we'd been the ones to see the three golden rainbows!"

Tashi grinned down at them. Then, at a word from Lama Kewtsang, they clattered out of the courtyard to begin their long search.

First came Lama Kewtsang on his big white horse, next came his assistant, then came Norbu the yak, laden down with baggage and, last of all, came Gen-la and Tashi.

They rode out of the city and soon the shining gold roofs of the temples of Lhasa had vanished in the haze behind them. At midday, Lama Kewtsang ordered a stop and Gen-la led the way to a little stream that ran by the

side of the road. Here, they set the horses and Norbu free to drink from its ice-cold waters.

After they'd eaten, Tashi helped pile the baggage on to Norbu's back again. On the very top of the load, Gen-la placed a carved wooden box with a heavy brass padlock and set about tying it on.

"What's in that box, Gen-la, and why is it locked?" Tashi asked. Gen-la looked at him steadily as he tied the last knots.

"Tashi," he said. "When the right time comes, I will ask you to bring this box to me and we will unlock it. But for now, no one must see what's inside it."

They stopped late that night and set off again early the next day.

On they rode.

As the afternoon of the second day wore on, and still they rode, Tashi grew very tired. "When are we going to stop for the night?" he asked.

Gen-la looked round at him. "I know you're tired, Tashi," he said, "but every day will not be as long as this one. Lama Kewtsang wants to reach the sacred lake of Lhamoi Latso before night falls — we're nearly there now."

"The sacred lake of Lhamoi Latso?" Tashi repeated. "We're going there?" All the people of Tibet knew about this lake whose waters had the power to reflect the future.

"Yes, Tashi," Gen-la replied. "We will camp for the night by the sacred lake of Lhamoi Latso. Who knows, maybe the lake will show us a sign to help us in our search."

As the sun set behind them, the full moon rose in the
eastern sky. The little search-party climbed yet another
hill — and there below them lay the sacred lake of Lhamoi
Latso.

In the moonlight, they set up their tents and cooked
their evening meal. Then Lama Kewtsang went into his
tent to pray that the lake would show them a sign to help
them on their way. By now, Tashi was very weary, but
before he fell asleep he too prayed for a sign.

When morning came, he peered out of the tent then made his way through swirling clouds of mist to the water's edge. Here, he could see more clearly. The lake was like a mirror — but all it reflected was the snowcapped mountain on the other side. Tashi gazed and gazed into the water, but the lake would tell him nothing.

He wandered slowly back to the camp, hoping the others would be up by now. As he got closer, he saw Gen-la bending over the little iron stove and called out to him.

Gen-la looked up. "As soon as we've eaten we'll be on our way again. Get yourself ready for the journey and, while you're waiting for breakfast, eat these." He handed him a fistful of dried apricots.

While Tashi waited, he wandered round the camp munching on the tangy apricots.

Then suddenly above him came a flapping of wings and a harsh squawking sound. He looked up just as a large black crow swooped down and landed on his shoulder.

The big bird stared at him with his greedy, yellow eye.

"Do you want food, crow?" Tashi asked, and offered a piece of apricot.

The bird shook his head.

"*Ah . . . Ka . . . Ma . . .*"

"*Ah . . . Ka . . . Ma . . . ?*" Tashi repeated in astonishment. Ah, ka and ma were three letters of the Tibetan alphabet! He walked slowly over to Gen-la with the crow perched on his shoulder.

"Gen-la," he said very quietly so as not to frighten the bird off. "Listen to this crow — he can talk!"

Gen-la looked up from his cooking and smiled.

The crow looked straight at him, then opened his beak. "*Ah . . . Ka . . . Ma . . . ,*" he croaked again and flapped off into the sky.

"*Ah . . . Ka . . . Ma . . .*" Gen-la echoed as his eyes
followed the crow's flight. He looked at Tashi. "We have
been given another sign."

After breakfast, they saddled the horses, loaded up
Norbu the yak and set off up the hill away from the sacred
lake.

When they got to the top, Tashi turned and looked
back. Now, a light breeze ruffled the surface of the lake
and, high above, flew the crow. Faintly, he heard, "*Ah . . .
Ka . . . Ma . . .*"

They kept their eyes on the bird until it was just a speck
in the sky. Then Gen-la turned to Tashi.

"Two years ago, the Regent came to this lake to pray
for a sign. He prayed for two whole days. Just when he had
nearly given up hope, a breeze sprang up and the surface
of the lake turned suddenly white. When the waters

cleared, the letters Ah, Ka and Ma appeared.''

"*Ah . . . Ka . . . Ma . . .*!'' Tashi exclaimed. "But those
are the letters the crow was saying!''

"I know,'' Gen-la replied. "But let me finish telling
you . . . As the letters faded, the Regent saw in the waters

of the lake the image of a monastery with a roof of green and gold. And from this monastery a twisting path led up the mountain to a little house with blue jade tiles and a flowering peachtree."

"But where *is* this house?" Tashi demanded.

"We do not know yet," was Gen-la's answer. "All we know is — we must follow the signs."

27

After leaving the sacred lake, the search-party set off
along the road to the north-east.

"How far do we have to go?" Tashi asked.

"We do not know," Gen-la replied. "All we can do is

follow the signs that will lead us to this child.''

And so on they rode — over plains, up through high mountain passes, across bridges made of rope and bamboo sticks and down again on to the plains. And always, they rode in the same order — first Lama Kewtsang on his big white horse, then his assistant, then Norbu laden down with baggage and last of all Gen-la and Tashi.

Not a day went by that they didn't meet up with other travellers on the road — sometimes merchants on their way to Lhasa, sometimes pilgrims and sometimes nomads with their herds.

Every day before they set off, Gen-la would load the baggage on to Norbu's broad back. And, always, he would check that the carved wooden box was tied on very tightly.

"When will you tell me what's in the wooden box?" Tashi often asked, and Gen-la's answer was always the same, "I will tell you when the time is right."

"And when will that be?" Tashi would murmur to himself, for sometimes he felt that he might spend the rest of his life riding towards the north-east and never getting anywhere . . .

29

One day, the search-party met two travellers on the road and stopped to talk.

"Where are you from?" Lama Kewtsang asked.

"We come from the mountains high up in the north-east," came the reply.

"Then maybe you can help us," Gen-la said. "We have travelled from Lhasa in search of a monastery with a roof of green and gold. From this monastery, a twisting path leads up to a house with blue jade tiles and a flowering peachtree."

The travellers glanced at each other, then one of them spoke. "We come from the province of Amdo, and it is there that you will find the monastery with the green and gold roof."

"But what about the house with the blue jade tiles and the flowering peachtree?"

"Oh, we know nothing about that." The man shrugged and without another word the two travellers continued on their way.

A little while later, the search-party crossed into Amdo province and began the long climb up into the mountains. As the afternoon wore on, their shadows lengthened and presently the sun set behind the snowcapped mountains.

"We will make our camp for the night soon —" Gen-la was saying, when he suddenly pulled up his horse. Directly in their path stood a young man.

"Where did *he* come from?" Gen-la wondered out loud, for a moment ago there'd been no one at all on the road. "We will ask him if he knows the house with the blue jade tiles," he whispered. As they drew closer to the young man he stopped and asked, "Can you help us please?"

"I will if I can," the young man replied.

"We are merchants," Gen-la explained, "and we have come from Lhasa in search of a monastery with a green and gold roof and a house with blue jade tiles."

"Then you have come to the right place," the young man replied. "Soon you will see the monastery with the green and gold roof — its name is Karma Rolpai Dorje. From the monastery, a twisting path leads up to the village of Takster, and there you will find the house with the blue jade tiles."

Gen-la looked at Lama Kewtsang, who gave a slight nod. "Thank you," he said. "You have been most helpful."

They rode on. When Tashi looked back the young man had vanished just as suddenly as he'd appeared. Gen-la did not seem at all surprised at this.

As the horses clopped their way along, the sound of the hooves on the stony ground made a rhyme start up in Tashi's head. "AM-do KA-MA, AM-do KA-MA" it went, and presently he began to sing the rhyme out loud.

"What are you singing?" Gen-la asked him.

"Just the rhyme the horses' hooves are saying," he explained.

"AM-do KA-MA. . .AM-do KA-MA. . . 'Amdo' for the province we're in and 'ka-ma' for Karma Rolpai Dorje monastery."

On they went, Tashi singing his song in time to the clopping of the horses' hooves and Gen-la riding along beside him deep in thought . . .

"Tashi!" he said suddenly and Tashi stopped his song. "Do you remember that crow at the sacred lake?"

"Of course I do!" Tashi replied. Who could forget a bird like that.

"What did the crow say to you?"

"*Ah . . . Ka . . . Ma . . .*" Tashi replied and then, "but that's just like my song of the horses' hooves."

"Exactly," replied Gen-la. "And those are the letters — Ah, Ka and Ma — that the Regent saw in the waters of the sacred lake."

Then they said together, "We really *are* on the right track!"

They made their way just a little further along the path. Soon Lama Kewtsang called a halt and Gen-la set up camp for the night. He unloaded the baggage from Norbu's back and carried the carved wooden box to the tent. As he gently laid it on the ground he said to Tashi, "Tomorrow. . ."

Early next morning Tashi helped Gen-la load the baggage on to Norbu's back and they set off up the mountain. Now, the search-party travelled in silence — for they knew they were nearing the end of their journey.

They rounded a curve in the path, then stopped —

34

dazzled by the shining green and gold roof of a large monastery.

Gen-la jumped off his horse and went up to a lama who was working outside. After speaking with him for a moment he returned.

"Yes, this is the monastery of Karma Rolpai Dorje," he announced, "and beyond it lies the village of Takster. We must follow the twisting path." He pointed to the side of the main monastery building. Sure enough, a narrow path led past it and up the hill. Gen-la looked at Lama Kewtsang, who nodded.

As they plodded up the path, Tashi could hear Norbu
puffing and panting as he trudged along with his heavy
load.

"Keep your strength just a little longer, my friend,
we're nearly there!" he called out to him.

They followed the path a short way further and soon the
village of Takster came into view.

Straight in front of them stood a little house. The edges of its flat roof were lined with blue jade tiles and by its side grew a flowering peachtree.

Prayer flags fluttered from a pole in the courtyard and a large dog was tied up by the door.

As they drew closer to the house, Lama Kewtsang ordered them to dismount and tether their horses. Then Gen-la took a small jug from the baggage on Norbu's back.

"What are you going to do?" Tashi asked.

"I will knock on the door and ask for some hot water for our tea," Gen-la replied.

They watched, hardly daring to breathe, as he walked towards the house, then they sighed with relief as his knock was answered.

A woman opened the door and Gen-la held up the jug. The woman nodded and smiled, then beckoned them all to come inside.

As they crowded into the little house, Tashi's heart was beating so loudly he felt the woman must surely hear it. But she didn't seem to, and just asked them all to sit down while she made some tea.

When his eyes got used to the darkness of the room, he noticed a little boy playing quietly in the corner. The child looked up at Tashi but went on with his game until his mother spoke to him. "Lamo Dontrub, our guests are merchants who have stopped at our house for a rest on their way".

At this, Lamo Dontrub stopped his game and stood up. Going straight over to Lama Kewtsang, he gazed up at him and said in a clear voice, "You are not a merchant!"

Lama Kewtsang's face did not change expression. He looked down at the child and asked, "Well, if I'm not a merchant, who am I?"

"You are a lama from Lhasa," the child announced calmly.

Lama Kewtsang drew in his breath sharply, then stepped forward to the boy's mother who stood staring at her son in astonishment.

"You must excuse us. The boy is right. We are not merchants, we are lamas. We have travelled from Lhasa in search of a special child, and our search has led us to this house." With these words, he took off his furry hat. When his assistant and Gen-la did the same and the woman saw they all had shaven heads, she knew her son had spoken the truth.

As the search-party settled down to drink their tea, Lamo Dontrub's mother went to call his father in from the fields.

After Gen-la had introduced Lama Kewtsang and explained why they were there, the boy's father said, "Lamo Dontrub has always been a most unusual child, and we have often wondered if he might have a special life ahead."

Lama Kewtsang then asked permission to question the boy.

"Of course," replied his parents. "This is a great honour for us."

Gen-la turned to Tashi and said, "The time has come to open the locked wooden box, Tashi. Come with me."

Together, they crossed the yard to Norbu and the horses. Gen-la untied the ropes that bound the baggage and lifted down the box.

"In this box," he said to Tashi, "are two strings of prayer beads, two small drums and two walking sticks. One of each belonged to our thirteenth Dalai Lama. If Lamo Dontrub can pick out the correct beads, drum and walking stick, then we will know that he is the child we are searching for."

They carried the wooden box into the house and placed it on the table. Gen-la handed Tashi the key.

Too excited to speak, he unlocked the box. Gen-la sat down, opened the lid and took out the two strings of prayer beads, the two small drums and the two walking sticks. Carefully, he placed them on the table.

Lamo Dontrub watched all this with great interest and even climbed up on to Gen-la's lap to get a better look.

Once there, he reached out and grasped one of the strings of beads. Looking at it closely, he exclaimed, "But this is *mine!*" and he turned to look straight at Gen-la.

"What are you doing with my beads?" he asked.

Next, he picked up one of the little drums. "This is mine, too," he remarked with a smile.

Then he took a long look at the two walking sticks. "And this belongs to me too!" he cried, picking up one and waving it in the air.

Lama Kewtsang looked across at Gen-la and nodded. "The child is right," he announced.

Many months went by. At last, the time came to begin the long journey back to Lhasa. As he mounted his horse, Gen-la looked out over the crowd that filled the village of Takster and turned to Tashi. "Remember how we came to this village — just four merchants from Lhasa with our yak?"

Tashi smiled. Now more than fifty men and their horses, mules and yaks waited to set off along the twisting path with Lamo Dontrub. On the long journey to Lhasa he would ride in a special carriage on the backs of two mules with his family riding close behind.

The procession was soon winding its way down the mountain, out of Amdo province, across rivers and over plains. As the weeks went by, more and more people joined it and each village they passed through honoured them with food and gifts.

At last, Gen-la said to Tashi, "Soon we will be met by the Regent and the official welcoming party for we are nearing Lhasa. Today, I want you to ride close to Lamo Dontrub and help him if he needs you for, as you know, he is very young . . ."

Tashi's heart leapt for joy. "Thank you, Gen-la," he replied, his eyes shining.

By mid afternoon they could see the shining gold roofs of distant Lhasa and carried on the breeze came the sound of joyful drums and bells.

Led by the official welcome party, a great crowd of people came thronging towards them.

They stopped and in a special ceremony Lamo Dontrub was proclaimed the fourteenth Dalai Lama. He was dressed in special robes and placed inside a gilded carriage filled with silken cushions.

From now on, the crowds swelled round the procession

and as they entered the city of Lhasa, thousands of
chanting lamas with brightly coloured banners lined the
way. All the people of Lhasa, young and old, came out in
their best clothes to pay homage and the air was filled with
the sound of horns and flutes and drums and cymbals.
Everyone was singing and dancing and some were crying
with joy.

As the trumpets and drums and bells rang out over the
city, the people twirled huge umbrellas and cried,
"The day of our happiness is come!"

47